Contents

THE ART OF COMMUNICATION

The visual arts are one of the most powerful means of human communication. They can uplift, disturb, challenge and provoke. They can lead us to view the world and our place in it in a new light. And whatever their impact, it is one which can endure for centuries.

BT makes communication possible across the length and breadth of the globe, across time and space. Through its sponsorship of National Touring Exhibitions, BT is helping to bring art of high quality within reach of communities throughout the UK. BT will open new doors to enable even more people to experience and appreciate art and enhance communication

NATIONAL TOURING EXHIBITIONS *Sponsored by* **BT**
ORGANISED BY THE SOUTH BANK CENTRE
FOR THE ARTS COUNCIL OF GREAT BRITAIN

In Fusion

NEW EUROPEAN ART

Ben Bella

Carlos Capelán

Benni Efrat

Chohreh Feyzdjou

Claudio Goulart

Ying Liang

Lea Lublin

As M'Bengue

Flavio Pons

Felix de Rooy

Ohannes Tapyuli

The South Bank Centre/Ikon Gallery 1993

Exhibition Tour

IKON GALLERY , BIRMINGHAM
27 February – 3 April 1993

BRIGHTON MUSEUM AND ART GALLERY
24 April – 30 May 1993

ORIEL AND CHAPTER, CARDIFF
26 June – 31 July 1993

A National Touring Exhibition sponsored by BT,
and organised in collaboration with Ikon Gallery

Exhibition curated by Gavin Jantjes, Elizabeth
Macgregor and Roger Malbert, assisted by Julia Coates
and Helen Juff

Catalogue designed by A. Arefin
Printed in England by Pale Green Press
© The South Bank Centre 1993
ISBN 1 85332 100 1

A full list of Arts Council and South Bank Centre
publications may be obtained from:
Art Publications,
South Bank Centre,
Royal Festival Hall,
London SE1 8XX

front cover: **Carlos Capelán** *Installation* (detail) 1992
back cover: **Ben Bella** *Crate Paint* 1975

Foreword

This exhibition brings together eleven artists who live and work in Europe but whose cultural roots are elsewhere in the world. Planned to coincide with the removal of trade barriers within the Community, its purpose is to affirm the diversity of Europe's cultures and to welcome the contribution of artists who do not fit neatly into the standard national or regional categories.

National identity remains an implicit theme of many art exhibitions circulated internationally; this is not surprising when they are organised or funded by national agencies and institutions whose raison d'être is precisely to promote a national culture. That there is a politics (not to mention an economics) of distribution of art on the international circuit, determining which artists are shown, is frequently forgotten.

Defining artists by nationality is often a dubious business in any case. The history of the twentieth century is, to an unprecedented degree, the history of migration and displacement, and this is conspicuously true in the arts. How many of the Western world's most eminent artists in this century have chosen, for one reason or another, to lead their lives in countries other than the land of their birth? Such movement and exchange are vital sources of stimulation to cultural life, and this is one good reason for welcoming the opening of national frontiers within Europe. A freer traffic of art and ideas with our neighbours can only be healthy.

However, Europe cannot be considered in isolation, its history is inextricably bound up with that of the wider world. The complexity of this history is reflected, in many ways, in the diversity of its minority populations. Yet as the internal borders of the Community are opened, a corresponding closure and tightening of restrictions on the outer peripheries is taking place, and this begs many questions.

Although it would have been logical to include in this exhibition artists living in Britain, it was felt that in a show of this scale it would be more valuable to provide an opportunity to see unfamiliar work from abroad. Most of the artists have never been shown before in Britain and some of the work has been made specially for the exhibition. Their birthplaces range from Africa and China to South America and their adopted cities include Paris, Amsterdam and Hamburg.

The initial research for the exhibition was undertaken at the invitation of the Ikon Gallery by Gavin Jantjes and we thank him for this and for his contributions to the catalogue. Among the people who assisted in his research and in the later stages of organising the show we would like especially to thank the following: Caroline Andrieux, L'Hôpital Ephémère; Albert Benamou Galeries; Professor K. P. Brehmer, Hochschule für Bildende Künste; Robert Darroll; Catherine David; Galerie Patricia Dorfmann; Professor H. El Attar, Projektgruppe Stoffwechsel; Dr Michael Haerdter, Künstlerhaus Bethanien; Pierre Hivernat, Attaché Culturel, Ambassade de France; Noha Hosni, L'Institut du Monde Arabe; Balraj Khanna; Sputnik Kilambi, Radio France; Henry Kol, the Royal Netherlands Embassy; Charlotte Malcolm-Smith; Jack Mensink, Stichting Kunst Mondial, Tilburg; Uwe Mokry, Galerie Basta; Els van der Plas, the Gate Foundation; Felix de Rooy; Jean Toppazzini; Dr Beate Winkler-Pohler; M. Catherine de Zegher.

The exhibition is presented with support from the Cultural Service of the French Embassy, A.F.A.A. (Association Française d'Action Artistique), Ministère des Affaires Etrangères and the Royal Netherlands Embassy.

HENRY MEYRIC HUGHES
Director of Exhibitions, The South Bank Centre

ELIZABETH A MACGREGOR
Director, Ikon Gallery

ROGER MALBERT
Exhibition Organiser

Ben Bella

LANGUAGE LESSON The name is caught in a fractured history. There is an aftertaste of a political past. Exiled. To be born a second time, elsewhere, into a life of resistance and revolt, a life woven of inward words and of far-off beings.

IMMIGRANT WORKER Another injury that the young Mahdjoub Ben Bella attributes to his original culture. In choosing, by his apprenticeship in the fine arts in France, to follow a foreign way of thinking and practising, he tries to locate and to inscribe on canvas the passage of a liberty which is untainted by treachery or abandonment. The schools will provide no shelter; there is only a solitary (which is not to say isolated) way out.

MOTHER TONGUE To search for a way out, for Mahdjoub Ben Bella, means to create an identity in order to communicate through art: to live, love, suffer, desire, from a position somewhere between two cultures, one of which is redundant and damaged, as far as the archetypal and maternal solace of writing is concerned. A calligraphic investigation which, with a wave of the hand, has the power to create or destroy the life which flows through it. This blood is inky-black.

CHOICE 'Intelligible' writing is that which most of us use daily, utilising agreed signs and symbols, quantified and qualified, in order to project our common humanity, our actions and thoughts in words. These symbols accord with the quasi-immutable order of language, with its conventions and dictates.

But there also exists, right alongside it, that abstract writing which the hand of Ben Bella traces, lets run quickly or slowly, with downstrokes and upstrokes, sounds and silences, voids and colours. Waves of writing which revive the memory of the mother-tongue, lost yet nevertheless tattooed in the marks of his script. (Listen to this overflowing speech which no longer belongs to reality but to painting, territory of the amnesia of cultures!)

LAYERS This form of voluntary illegibility which Ben Bella has invented refers only to itself. Writing relearns colour. The speech unwinds itself, agitated by the scars of memory. Is this a form of tattoo?
Archaeology: where do traces begin? Where do they end? Those who cannot forget will never finish drawing the unthinkable past.

AFFINITIES Ben Bella tells me that he has forgotten the Arabic language. (At heart, I doubt it.)
Through its conjugations, the French language, in contrast to the Arabic, has established an oppressive tense: the 'passé simple'. Ben Bella is the narrator-author who abolishes our 'passé simple'.

EBB AND FLOW I sense that there are other affinities in the script of Ben Bella. Music – another side of the silence of his work. The rhythms of ink are recitations evoking choral voices. Bach certainly plays a part in this painting, as do those contemporary composers whose musical scores Ben Bella has sometimes distorted in order to invent visual movements from them, subverting the alignment of the staves. Carrying with him only the essential is a mark of the nomad: musical language is essential. A fugue of signs.
The writing 'peddled' by Ben Bella is not a form of automatism. It's the writing of a body poised for an instant in the ebb and flow of the shifting appearances of reality. It is anarchic, existing for the look and no longer for the thought. Expressions of a subjectivity of which it is all the less sure as it desires the more ardently to be 'understood' and 'recognised' by the Other.
There was even a day (was it in Tourcoing or Arras?) when it began raining derisory signs on the northern pavements. Do you remember ...?

ALAIN MACAIRE
Translated from the French by Leigh Markopoulos.

right: **Ben Bella**
Painted Writing (detail) 1991

Ben Bella
Painted Writing 1991

Ben Bella
Painted Writing 1991

Carlos Capelán

What strikes the viewer when looking at an installation by Carlos Capelán is the sensation of being in the presence of a ritualistic process that is taking shape, without a precise beginning or end. One expects the artist to be there still, working it out.

His powerful drawings made with mud, sand or ink; the stones and rocks; the stacks of eroded, rescued or burned old textbooks; the elements of furniture; they all seem part of a continuum. The drawings spread up and down a wall, across a floor, drifting into corners and onto the ceiling. It is as though Capelán is driven to leave his mark on everything.

Carlos Capelán's life is as complex and multifaceted as his work. As a young man he was forced to leave Uruguay because he was committed to fighting totalitarianism and opposed the outrageous injustices, torture and systematic silencing which awaited anyone who resisted the fascist oriented government.

After leaving Uruguay, he became a political organiser in Chile while the government of Salvador Allende was in power. He was imprisoned and nearly killed when Allende was overthrown, but was given asylum in Sweden, where he now lives.

Capelán's imagery seems to resist definition, or translation into words. His obsessive linear drawing, however, renders these images as writing, as a score, or as a diary. One follows the handprints and fingerprints going over the surface of the wall, paper or any material he chooses, like skin that is being tattooed.

Everything in his work is closely connected to the special condition of being an Uruguayan exile living in Sweden. Instead of assimilating to his new environment, or hanging on to some notion of a Latin-American minority in exile, an exotic 'Other', he has opted for another strategy. Aware that the 'mainstream' may define his work in relation to its own references and discourse, Capelán twists the stratagem by utilising these references in his creative landscape.

Another concern is the notion that the repetition of certain figures turns them into signs or icons, as in the mass media, or even baroque art, creating a more conceptual framework. Those images seem to have been with us forever in much the same way as certain thoughts and ideas have always been in our memory, since we have all been 'exiled' from our past to some extent. In exile, the surroundings are perceived to change but memory remains constant, repeating itself over and over.

Capelán uses earth from all over the world. The earth is one of the most powerful means of association with nature: it brings to mind femininity, the obscure and interior space which constitutes the originating and germinating force. He couples this with ashes, which he sees as part of a Latin-American landscape where one is constantly in touch with the energies of those who were before us, those who left behind something like 'Memorias del Fuego' (Memories of Fire).

The old textbooks, a cultural testament, appear in stacks held down by the weight of a rock, like small devotional and ritualistic monuments seen in the countryside.

On the walls Capelán inscribes quotations from books, magazines, proverbs, art history, anthropology, sociology and friends, onto surfaces of earth, mud and pigment. The lighting is like the anonymous, cheap, mass-produced reading lamps found everywhere, from homes in rural areas, to the hidden offices of any Latin-American secret police.

The totality of these elements becomes like a living map, one that acts provocatively as a global vision of culture, where local and regional projects are conducting a dialogue with modernist premises. Capelán reveals a Latin-American consciousness that moves on the border between the Western notion of 'Ego' and the 'Other', the otherness of magical ethnicity.

CARLA STELLWEG

right: **Carlos Capelán**
Painting on Map 1992

11

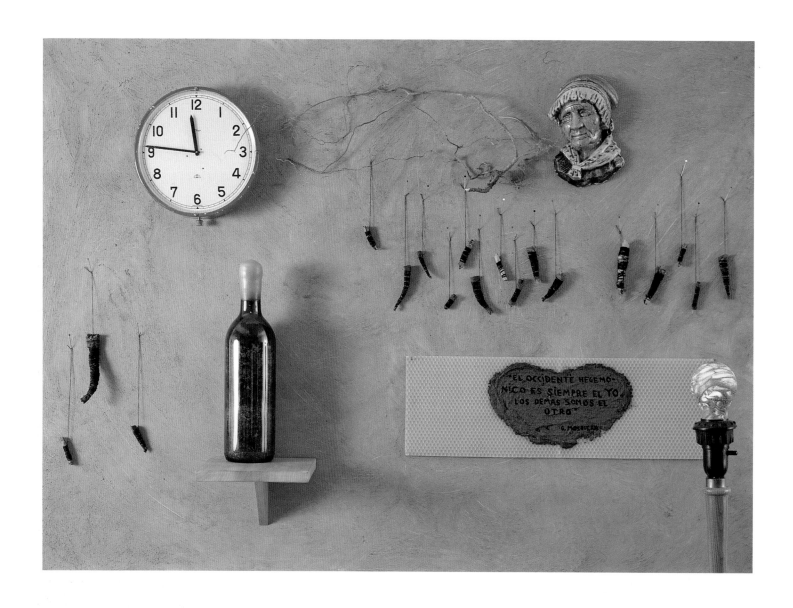

Carlos Capelán
Installation (detail) 1992

Carlos Capelán
A Bride of the... 1992

13

Benni Efrat

ARARAT EXPRESS, SUMMER 2034

This work by Benni Efrat, realised in 1986 on the occasion of the 'Octobre des Arts' in Lyons, France, is actually conceived not as a tape to be projected on stationary monitors, but rather to be carried on horseback through a certain location. The subject-matter of the videotapes consists of migrations and dispersals: people on the move, refugees, hoards of animals, streams of disoriented people, ambulances, boat people drowning, etc. Although the subject-matter of these films coincides with the manner in which they are displayed (a caravan of horses with video screens mounted both sides of the saddle) and the syntax of the work can thus rightly be called tautological, it shows anything but the tautological emptiness of 'art about art'. Quite the contrary; it is not self-referential, but refers to the world outside the work of art. It implies that the author is taking a stance; ecological disasters and demographic cataclysms seem so imminent to him that any autistic concentration on art (art about art) seems a mere perversion. His other – sculptural and graphic – works also deal with ecological/demographic reality and the problems of life at the end of the twentieth century. However, Efrat reflects on these issues as if in retrospect, from some fifty years ahead.

Ararat Express refers to the archetypal story of the Deluge: the great moral cleansing at the time of Noah, which guaranteed the continuation of animal and human life on earth. Since the story of Noah is essentially a moral story, Efrat's work suggests that morality nowadays is about protecting, saving and managing the earth and its population. Sin is no longer to do with the strict observance of rigorous religious codes, but rather concerns the awareness of the fact that the earth is entrusted to us; it is our responsibility to maintain it.

Art has always tried to 'freeze' a consensus view of the cultural status quo at any time – hence the preference for stone and other resistant materials. Art consolidates that which is considered to be meaningful and passes it on to future generations. Video reflects the dynamism characteristic of our time. Efrat does not employ a static presentation of moving images, but comes closer to the essence of his underlying subject-matter by introducing the concept of motion, of being on the road and migrating, within the very structure and form of display of this work. The curious juxtaposition of images and the apparent contrast between high-tech electronics and time-honoured means of transport (horseback), make *Ararat Express, Summer 2034* a fascinating, sufficiently diverse yet internally coherent work of art and a powerful statement on what art is about in our time.

YONAH FONCE-ZIMMERMAN
Curator MUHKA - Museum van Hedendaagse Kunst, Antwerp.

right: **Benni Efrat**
Ararat Express Oct. 2043 1986

above & right: **Benni Efrat**
Ararat Express Oct. 2043 1986

Chohreh Feyzdjou

THE BAZAARS OF BABEL

However one approaches it and whatever one's first response – whether to the radical and violent confusion of the studio or the more analytical arrangements of the photographs or the gallery installation – the work of Chohreh Feyzdjou displaces and disconcerts our usual landmarks. A first impression derived from certain immediately apparent elements (accumulation, repetition, the colour black, the precise arrangements of rolls of paper, boxes, jars, bags and crates), as much as from the order systematically imposed on the objects, invites two ostensibly opposed, indeed contradictory, readings, depending on one's interpretation of the phrase 'Product of Chohreh Feyzdjou'. It could on the one hand be a critique of the art of the commercial era, of bland aestheticism and the never-ending trade in objects and signs, the era of consumerism (the 'product of'). Alternatively, it could be a

representation of the 'Other', the exotic and hermetic discourse of 'Chohreh Feyzdjou', the Iranian artist living and working in Paris for the last 15 years, whose own culture borrows from the traditions of the Muslim East, from Judaism and the West.

But these two cautious first attempts at interpretation do not so much shed light on the work and the complex cultural operations apparent in it, as highlight the inadequacy of the models we have to help us analyse and comprehend forms produced on the fringe or periphery of the 'agreed' centres of modernity. At the end of this century, in this paradoxical era of the 'global village' and of the withdrawal into the self, of nationalistic awakenings and crises of identity, but also of the questionable promotion of the idea (and the by-products) of 'world culture', the time seems to have come for another more attentive and imaginative culture, for multiple exchanges between the ancient and new

centres and peripheries of Western culture, between tradition and modernity, between mother-countries and (ex)colonies, for very different exchanges that go beyond the classical notion of 'influences'. In literature, music and the visual arts, it is the unfinished history of 'acculturations' and of syncretisms which must be envisaged today, as well as the history of subjects irreducible to single ethnic, economic and geographic determinisms. This history is complex, divided and plural, like the diasporic, refugee-like, exiled and migrant reality of too many modern populations.

In this context of lost or shattered cultures (her own but also ours), Chohreh Feyzdjou works patiently and methodically on her 'black magic', a contemporary alchemy of the only sort which is possible today, ironical and disenchanted. With wax, the colour black, feathers and hair, she concocts unsettling artefacts, multiplies incomplete inventories and mutilated

assemblages; she uses collections of signs, of meanings, of objects hoarded in the studio or installed in the gallery, evoking the chaos of the cellar or a chamber of horrors or an old curiosity shop. Remnants, fragments and scraps whose origins and functions are now irretrievable, they seem born, like the monsters of mythology, from the 'sleep of reason' and the nightmares to which it gives birth.

But the effacing of landmarks, the migration and unbounded wandering of men, things and signs also produce new structures, original syntaxes. It hardly matters whether they depend on tradition or modernity, the East or the West, the rhetoric of the installation or the confusion of the bazaar. In the violent collision of forms and traditions, a poetic as much as a historical intuition is expressed, tying together memory and the present, with the gesture of the passer-by, 'not reconciled', but with no trace of nostalgia for the past. The rolls of

painting are laid out and cut up by the metre, like common oilcloths, but the numerous stitched canvases which make them up are inaccessible to the enquiring eye and hand, like the sacred coils and texts of Judaism. The subtle dialectic of display and concealment no longer depends on respect for clearly understood laws, but on a spectacle transferred to the video screen where we see the inner surface of the rolls methodically unravelled.

In a text evaluating the interest, but also the risks, presented by the spread of Simultaneous Translation between the different cultures of the world in our modern Babel, a system which would rather sacrifice the necessarily conflicting diversity of multiple traditions to the consensual ideal of a 'common language', the Indian essayist Homi Bahbha wrote: 'Where once we could believe in the comfort and continuities of tradition, today we must face the responsibilities of cultural translation. In the attempts to mediate

between different cultures, languages and societies, there is always the threat of mistranslation, confusion and fear.'[1] At a time when many interests would like to promote an accessible universalism, a translation without errors but equally without trace of the original language, the work of Chohreh Feyzdjou comes to remind us that memory is the mocking, but irreplacable, fragile treasure of the passer-by.

CATHERINE DAVID

1. Homi Bhabha, 'Simultaneous Translation: Modernity and the Inter/National', *Expanding Internationalism*, Venice, 1990.

Extracted from the catalogue to the exhibition 'Products of Chohreh Feyzdjou 1988-1992', Galerie Patricia Dorfmann, Paris.

Translated from the French by Leigh Markopoulos.

Chohreh Feyzdjou
Products of Chohreh Feyzdjou 1988-1992 (details)

above & right: **Chohreh Feyzdjou**
Products of Chohreh Feyzdjou 1988-1992 (details)

20

Claudio Goulart

FIRST THOUGHTS We may know the facts but the way they are visually presented may deeply affect the way we understand them. And as time goes by what remains in our minds is an image, or an impression of images. Here, visual artists (and the film and television industry, the makers of our visual memory) play a significant role.

We may only guess the effect that the first images european artists made of America and other new found lands had at the time. A fantastic new world to the eyes of anyone who had the chance to be exposed to those images. They were an important source of information. On the other hand, most of the artists who made them never left Europe and consequently their production is saturated with idealisations and is on the border of if not pure fantasy. From today's perspective, those images tell us more about a way of seeing than what is being depicted.

For lack of visual records of the facts as they happened, idealisations and fantasies are used as a suitable substitute. For instance, the 19th-century painting The First Mass in Brazil, by Vitor Meirelles, is very often used in books to illustrate that historical event. All relevant information such as the time it was made is no longer important. Finally, we understand the event through that image.

The development of a new medium will not necessarily open up new possibilities, but it surely adds some new questions. The film Christopher Columbus (1949) is a reconstruction of the discovery of America in the idealised manner of paintings and engravings previously made on the subject. To stress its importance: it was until recently the only feature film made about that subject. The spectacular Conquest of Paradise (1992) is a more up-to-date account. However, there are no naked natives, which reminds us of some old questions. In both films the realism of the medium overpowers the historical perspective we may still have – when the lights of the projection room are turned off we experience those images as if we had been 'there'.

The same can be said about the Tarzan films of the Twenties and Thirties. They were the first images of Africa widely disseminated through the mass media. Though they were meant as pure entertainment, for millions these films were the main if not the only source of information about Africa. In Tarzan, the Ape Man (1932), the first with full sound, Jane's father, who has the authority of a scientific explorer, introduces her to the different tribes (back-projection) meeting in the marketplace. Original footage is used many times in Jane's unfolding adventure. It is remarkable how in sixty years of Tarzan films original footage from African natural and cultural life is mixed with strange animals, fantastic landscapes and wild people, so that we are left with the impression that it is all part of the same thing.

If in Tarzan films we still know that it is all an adventure, on television we find a more subtle situation. The recent 'discovery' of the Amazon and other rainforests by television brings the tropical jungle into millions of homes. Television representations of wilderness are intended to be as faithful as possible to reality. But the medium reduces everything that is presented to the same level of perception, and tropical jungles end up becoming relatively big gardens in the middle of civilisation.

Back to historical images, it is relevant to point out how europeans failed to comprehend the New World, and how the West still appropriates the 'exotic' to fulfil its need for fantasy and adventure – and to perpetuate a certain relationship. Furthermore many questions involving visual representation reflect (and cause and reflect again) deeper problems within a culture. The fear of the unknown is not only a problem for Western culture: when attempting to depict the new, often we find ourselves doing nothing more than mirroring our own prejudices and desires.

SECOND THOUGHTS Vale Quanto Pesa ('It's Worth Its Weight') is the brand name of a toilet soap. As a kid I used to wash my mouth out with it when I had told a lie. It is not easy to say the truth. Naturally for an artist it is not only a moral question but mainly an artistic one. As for the public, they can walk to the next picture or switch to the next channel. Not every image is worth a thousand words. Images can deceive us. We may like this way because we do not want to see the facts behind and the implications beyond.

CLAUDIO GOULART

23

Claudio Goulart
VALE QUANTO PESA
IT'S WORTH ITS WEIGHT (detail) 1993

Ying Liang

CIRCLES WITH FEET

Traditional Chinese ink painting is determined in choice of motif and depiction by a rigid rule system, behind which the individuality of the artist is forced to retreat. In order to look for breakaway alternatives to the strict conventions of her homeland, the Peking-born Ying Liang travelled to Hamburg in 1983 to study art.

These ink paintings were produced by the 31-year-old's intensive dialogue with her particular cultural sources – an artistic dialogue that would be unthinkable in conservative China. She playfully seizes on traditional motifs, and gives them a more personal expression by placing them in different contexts: the water-buffalo lies in the bathtub, the frog leaps into the jam, the circle with feet flies in front of a cricket.

Liang follows no predetermined concepts – she listens only to her intuition. In this way the break-up of the structures she has brought with her is not only an experimental end in itself, but also testifies to an inner rift, an uprooting following the separation from cultural roots and family. Contradictions run through the pictures: word-drawings without meaning, stamps without bureaucratic purpose, erotic allusions combined with force, touches of humour that seem to mask a deeper melancholy.

Conflict is also evident in the interpretation the works have been given: her deliberate use of symbolically powerful mythological elements is similar to that found in children's drawings, which unselfconsciously reveal information about their state of mind. Through her bold approach Liang gives aesthetic emphasis to empty spaces, in which she relates the graphic forms so as to stress the tension between them. She paints on traditional Chinese calligraphy paper, another aspect of her work that may not be immediately apparent to lestern eyes.

STEFAN BARTSCH

Translated from the German by Leigh Markopoulos. (With permission from the 'Hamburger Rundschau', 3 September 1992)

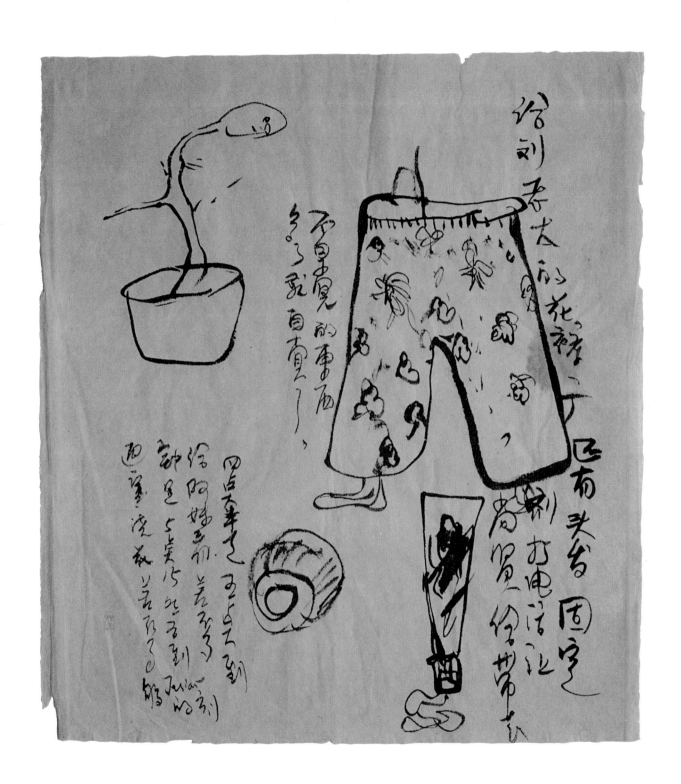

Ying Liang

Flowered pants for Mrs Liu 1990

Ying Liang
Untitled 1990

Ying Liang

My son will be a genius 1991

29

Lea Lublin

HOTEL DES ARTS

For over ten years, Lea Lublin has looked with an inquisitive eye at major works from the history of art, not with a sense of nostalgia, or, for that matter, to follow in the path of the appropriationists. Not content simply to copy the works, she has, rather, discovered in them hidden aspects that social convention keeps from us. In her 1983 show, Lublin unveiled the erotic charge that is immanent in the gestures of the Virgin and Child, by placing cut-out elements into reproductions of religious paintings and isolating significant scenes in drawings. Without any previous knowledge of Leo Steinberg's studies of the sexuality of Christ (Lublin met Steinberg subsequently in Paris, and he was astonished by the correspondences in their work), she brought forth visible signs of the masculinity of the child-God and the repressive space as well as projecting the forbidden desires of the artist.

Lublin's work, which is fundamentally Conceptual, posits an imaginative passage of appearances, rendering a new and additional meaning to iconic images, thus giving them new life. This is an intuitive and heuristic passage, which stems principally from the content of the art and from the discovery of the signified elements. If there is an accusatory attitude in Lublin's earlier pieces, in her new series, entitled *Présent suspendu* (*Suspended Present*, 1991), Lublin has created a work of allegiance to her spiritual father, Marcel Duchamp. Originally Argentinian, Lublin went to Buenos Aires following in Duchamp's footsteps to investigate his 1918-19 sojourn there. Lublin discovered some startling clues to his cryptic works. Working from Duchamp's correspondence with his family, she was able to locate his studio, which had a window with opaque panes, painted a yellowish green, perhaps the inspiration for Duchamp's 1920 *Fresh Widow*. Also, in a copy of *La Nacion* – a newspaper of the era almost certainly read by Duchamp – Lublin found an advertisement for Rose's Lime Juice, from which he may have taken his well-known feminine pseudonym, Rrose Selavy.

Lublin has transformed this Duchampian memoir into visual creations in a spectacular way, using new technological media that allow for seductive affective and formal analogies. Enlarged photographs of the studio inscribed with a circle, *Les Fenêtres Fraiches* (*The Fresh Windows*, 1990) evoke not only the famous 'window', but also the magnifying glass that Duchamp used in the execution of *A regarder (de l'autre côté du verre) d'un oeil, de près, pendant presque une heure* (To be looked at {from the other side of the glass} close to, for almost an hour, 1918), the label and the bottle of Rose's Lime Juice are used in a series of large computer images, and presented in light boxes, which give the found information a personal feeling, following the phenomenal number of variations on the Duchampian myth; thus, the label of *La bouteille perdue de Marcel Duchamp* (*The Lost Bottle of Marcel Duchamp*, 1991) reproduces the label of an assisted readymade: *Belle Haleine, Eau de Voilette* (*Beautiful Breath, Veil Water*, 1921) with the portrait and monogram of Rrose Selavy, modern Ariadne. Lublin unwinds her thread through the linguistic labyrinth of Duchamp's secrets, but she does not make readymades. In a manner that might be termed narrative, Lublin's work, in her own words, has nothing to do with 'the image as being reality, but as being reality of the image'.

Anne Dagbert

First published in Artforum, March, 1992

right: **Lea Lublin**
The Lost Bottle of Marcel Duchamp 1991

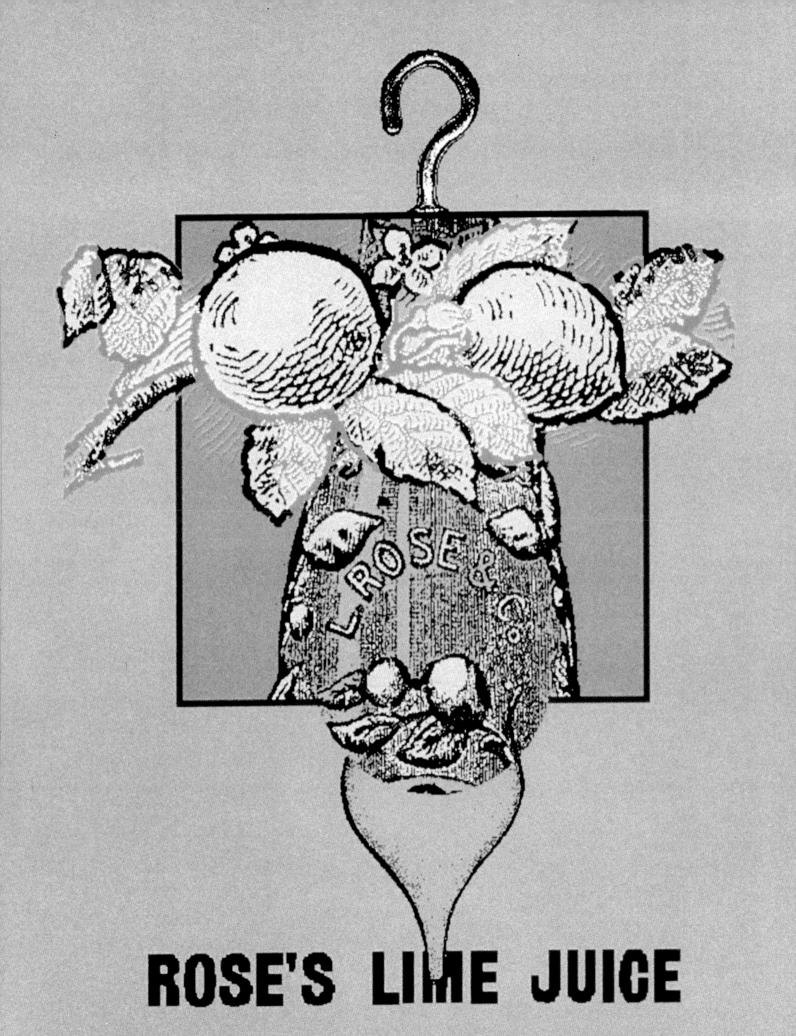

ROSE'S LIME JUICE

above & left: **Lea Lublin**
The Lost Bottle of Marcel Duchamp 1991

As M'Bengue

After Paris, New York, Munich, it is now the turn of cities in Britain to discover, before Tokyo and other capitals, the powerful canvases of As M'Bengue. From the beginning, this young Senegalese artist has demanded recognition, doubtless because the vigour and modernity of his painting touches a universal chord.

An African, Ibrahima As M'Bengue's work vibrates with the rhythm of the music of his continent: koras, balafons and tam-tams. In this respect he resembles his Senegalese compatriot the poet Leopold Sedar Senghor, who knows instinctively how to express in words the richness and depth of the many mysterious voices of Africa. But as a painter As M'Bengue is first of all a visual artist, and on his canvases he remakes the world. He transfigures it by playing with all the hues of his native country, all the ochres and maroons, the greys, reds and greens which evoke the powerful elements: Earth and Fire. And above all, the blues – those of the Air and the Water. The blue of the sea is present in all the paintings of As M'Bengue. Son of the great family of the Lébous, a maritime people who live by and for the ocean, As M'Bengue never fails to respect the family tradition, which he finds deeply moving: whenever he is returning to or leaving his homeland, he always goes with his mother to offer some sacrificial gifts to the hidden forces of the sea, the Djins.

Arriving in Paris in 1982, As M'Bengue, far from his roots, energetically entered into contact with the Western world. But he never let himself be dispossessed. On the contrary, he knew how to explore intelligently and how to appropriate the riches of that other culture and that other vision of the world. Moreover, his work, nourished by two sources, makes him fully aware of the multiplicity of human experience and the breadth of life, with its misfortunes and successes, love and hate, pleasure and sorrow, tears and laughter. One discovers in the texture of his works the mark of great symbols, and essential, timeless questions. From ritual initiations to sexual awakening, from the dramas of war, human folly and disease, to social or colonial injustice. The painting of As M'Bengue is an endless pursuit of truth through art.

JACQUES BOUZERAND

Translated from the French by Leigh Markopoulos.

As M'Bengue

Literary Library 1992

As M'Bengue

A Week of Kindness, or the Three Essential Elements of Max E 1992

As M'Bengue
The Misfortunes of the Immortals. 3 Free Men 1992

Flavio Pons

I deny that there are beautiful colours and ugly colours, beautiful shapes and others that are not. I'm convinced that any object, any place without distinction, can become a key of enchantment for the mind, according to the way one looks at it and the associations of ideas which one attaches to it. At this new level any evaluation of the work of art must take account not of its aesthetic "beauty" but of its greater or lesser capacity to stimulate the mind.

JEAN DUBUFFET

THEATRICAL RECYCLING?

Flavio Pons' recent works (shown under the title *Strange Fruits* in the Suzanne Biederberg Gallery in Amsterdam) are made of *objets trouvés*, which acquire a new place and meaning through the instinctive, surrealistic pleasure with which they are playfully combined. The artist takes revenge on the consumer's viewing habits, on the pretence of ownership. Yet his point of view is never moralising or polemical; it always remains cool and seductive. His way of showing used objects in installations is fascinating and the final effect of the close association between the objects is liberating, almost sarcastic.

One might speak of baroque theatre in this context, of the way in which it arouses our bewilderment, and also the sense in which it is an assemblage of different materials and iconographies; yet the stage setting is subtle, cerebral, static. This work affords a kind of neutral, restrained pleasure.

In the recycling process objects can still be identified, but their spatial relationships to each other and the strange combinations ironically force the viewer to alter his or her expectations. The viewer is forced not to get emotionally involved, despite the automatic personal associations which casually cross one's mind. Here the theatre is not internalised, but functions before our eyes as a mechanism, prepared to play the game for a moment; a moment which exorcises our merciless wish for death. Pons' visual strategy, in an elegant, intentionally naive manner, is to stage our habitual sadomasochistic relationship with things: a spectacular relationship.

GINO CALENDA

Flavio Pons
Solids (detail) 1992

Flavio Pons
Solids (detail) 1992

40

Flavio Pons
Solids 1992

Felix de Rooy

Felix de Rooy's collages and assemblages, which have not been exhibited publicly before, may be considered as a more personal expression of his concerns as a film director, a collector and curator. Born in Curaçao, in the Dutch Antilles, de Rooy lives in Amsterdam but in many ways it is the Caribbean that fires his vision. He returns to Curaçao frequently and has shot two of his feature films there – *Almacita Soul of Desolato* (1986) and *Ava & Gabriel* (1990) – using an almost entirely local cast and the vernacular, Papiamento. His collages seem to convey in a condensed form many of the most striking qualities of his films: the mood and atmosphere of the island, its brilliant light and the mysterious power of the landscape, as well as the religious intensity of the people.

In de Rooy's assemblages, social conflict and contradiction are expressed allegorically through disparate, even incompatible, elements placed in close relation: emblems of European trade, imperialism and the 'higher yearnings' of its civilisation combined with demeaning European images of black people, symbolic of domination and exploitation. The assemblages relate to the objects de Rooy has collected for the Negrophilia collection, an archive of 5,000 items of Western popular culture containing representations of black people from the mid-eighteenth century to the present day. The collection documents every racist stereotype, and is described by de Rooy as an aid to further discussion of race relations, providing historical insights that expose the underlying psychology of racialist attitudes.

There is a moment in de Rooy's film *Almacita Soul of Desolato* when an African woman is seen framed in an open doorway, stooping to pick up a bowl. An allusion to the seventeenth-century Dutch painter Pieter de Hooch, it surfaces here like an unexpected memory, and this conjunction of references epitomises the versatility and complexity of de Rooy's imagination. His collages contain similar contrasts – their mystical, apocalyptic imagery is contained within Dutch antique carved wooden frames. The mix is what defines de Rooy: the fusion of races in sex, the mixing of blood, religions, languages and cultures.

ROGER MALBERT

Visions from the entrails of human history – a multicoloured multiheaded monster devouring itself – a cannibalistic orgy to the rhythm of labour contractions – feeding on foetuses fermenting amidst blood and placenta the apocalyptical virus – the multi minority migrant society syndrome.

Fever, dreams cold sweat – newspaper ink spits stones from Rostock – a mosque explodes on digital T.V. – nationalism floats on waves of segregation – burns on L. A. home video – etched behind eyes with acid tears – the pilgrimage of the homeless for crumbs – crumbling under hungry rage – a miracle messiah murdered in a subway station.

Embrace sex and race – culture and religion rushing through my veins – history boiling a stew yet unnamed. Dine on memories of third world women raped by first world males – penetrating fortune and fame – erecting borderlines with second-hand shame.

Now he drapes her body inside me with couture of leather, silk and gold lamé – sways her pain away with a reggae lullaby – I insulate his heart with acid rock and hip-hop – drink solidarity blood from Wedgwood cups.

A vision born – a colonial orgasm torn from historical hypocrisy – cultural schizophrenia – religious insanity with the delicate balance of sexual duality – a universal identity set free.

FELIX DE ROOY

right: **Felix de Rooy**
Cry Surinam 1992

Felix de Rooy
Resurrection 1990

Felix de Rooy
Ave Europa Regina/White on Black 1991

Ohannes Tapyuli

Any German department store or shopping mall reveals what drives Tapyuli's artistic project. The consumers' desires of this most affluent post-war European economy, their longing for 'the good life', is the focus of his work. Tapyuli's position within this culture is ambivalent: he is constantly asking if he has become a part of it or has been made to stand apart from it. He believes that after more than twenty years he is a part of it, but a vital and critical part.

His work from the Seventies resonates with a sense of melancholy and loss of a homeland. Tapyuli's new work has moved from the large graphite drawings of suitcases, men waiting in railway stations and favourite pieces of furniture, to a new horizon. If the early work looked away from the Bundesrepublik and suggested nostalgia, the new 'object-boxes' comment on his immediate surroundings. The choice of materials and objects from popular culture emphasises that Tapyuli has come to terms with his new reality. By and large, he works with the waste materials of this affluent society. Wood, paper and cardboard destined for the rubbish heap are here transformed into works about desire. Tapyuli prefers the mail-order catalogue to fine art catalogue as a resource on German culture: rows of Meissner porcelain, deluxe washing machines, food and clothing become the signifiers of these desires.

He covers his box constructions with a layer of diffusion paper which makes the image elusive. One's view of reality is disturbed, the objects hide behind a smoke-screen and the desire to acquire is disrupted. One cannot desire what is undefined, one cannot possess a mirage. Tapyuli's translucent covering functions like the packaging of consumer produce, and makes the work speak about imagined possession and artifice. The constructions function like gifts, which the viewer has to unwrap intellectually, in order to discover the surprise they withhold.

Tapyuli's giant shirts (only six of the twelve are shown here) underline abundance and bourgeois grandeur by means of repetition and a false sense of scale. Those who desire to wear these colossal shirts are the Titans of our time. Fashion becomes a metaphor for the threat that the world is to be laid waste once again through the ambitious desires of humans straining for omnipotence. He calls his collection of shirts *We are Rich*. It reads like a tongue-in-cheek celebration of the desire of the well-off to go out and buy. It is a work which smiles knowingly at the inflated Biedermeier mentality of German contemporary culture. I say 'smiles' because Tapyuli is not a satirist: to ridicule their aspirations and laugh at them would indicate a lack of humility and understanding. Tapyuli is a protagonist questioning Germany's *Wegwerfgesellschaft* ('throw-away society'), a society which is driven to consume the new and which overlooks the posi-tive values of the old. How one chooses to define a 'better tomorrow' in Europe is overshadowed by a materialism which disrupts vision. Tapyuli finds his role as a visionary artist by making others recon-sider their relation to an endemic consumerism.

Gavin Jantjes

Ohannes Tapyuli
We Are Rich (studio shot) 1992

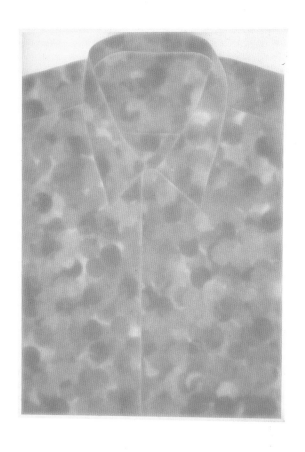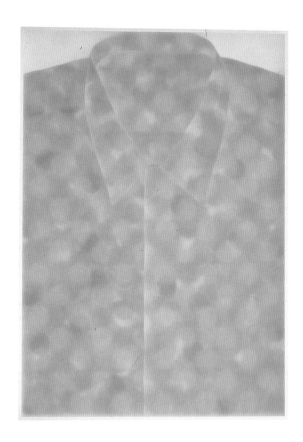

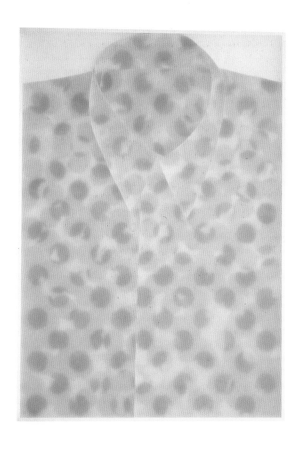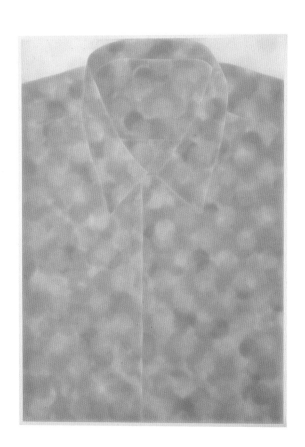

left & above: **Ohannes Tapyuli**
We are Rich 1992

Gavin Jantjes

Reconnoitre

A personal view

Festivals provide the arts with a peg on which to hang exhibitions. In 1992 the 500th anniversary of Columbus's voyage across the Atlantic was celebrated through many arts events, which provided an opportunity to contemplate, criticise and discuss the outward-looking spirit of the age of discovery. Columbus signifies Europe's desire to engage with 'otherness'; to involve itself with different peoples and cultures and to discover new things about the world. There are various historical readings in Europe and America of Europe's desire to engage and its ability to discover. The anniversary confronted us with many different interpretations.

In 1993 we are invited to celebrate 'open Europe'. The removal of the old internal boundaries of the Community must be welcomed. Europe wants to signal the creation of a new identity, which is characterised by a sense of cultural unity shared by all its citizens. 'In Fusion' is a part of these celebrations. Its aim is to examine Europe's newness in the context of cultural difference and diversity in the visual arts. The collapse of the post-war settlement in Eastern Europe and the challenge of post-modernist thought to the philosophy which underpinned modernism lend urgency to the task.

By the year 2000, it is estimated that there will be fifty million people with extra-European cultural roots living in Europe. Sixteen million already hold citizenship of a European state. How the identities of these 'new Europeans' are woven into the fabric of the nation states they live in, and European culture in general, has to be considered in the context of the 'open Europe' celebrations in 1993. Paul Ricoeur describes this challenge succinctly:

No one can say what will become of our civilisation when it has really met different civilisations by means other than the shock of conquest and domination. But we have to admit that this encounter has not yet taken place at the level of an authentic dialogue. That is why we are in a kind of lull or interregnum in which we can no longer practise the dogmatism of a single truth and in which we are not yet capable of conquering the scepticism into which we have stepped.[1]

The art of the 'new European' artists opens a debate about their cultural identity that Britain has been involved in for many years, and it has led to a more general recognition of the heterogeneity of this country's contemporary visual culture. Any account of British art of the Seventies is likely to include the names of Auerbach, Bacon, Freud, Kitaj and Paolozzi; in the Eighties it extends to Bhimji, Biswas, Boyce,

Hatoum, Houshiary, Kapoor, Piper and Rodney. The official recognition given these artists offers perhaps the only example within Europe which avoids paternalism and grapples with the scepticism mentioned by Paul Ricoeur.

By focussing on the achievements of artists living on the European mainland[2], 'In Fusion' increases our knowledge of the diversity and difference in contemporary art there. It also suggests possibilities for a redefinition of 'European' art of the Nineties.

In 1993 we can recognise that the 'newness' that European politicians speak of is an abstraction, particularly in the field of culture. Intellectuals talk idealistically of Europe being turned into a post-modern cultural space, where notions of ethnicity and cultural plurality coexist; this is an imagined alternative to the dominance of modernism, but the reality is very different. The celebrations of European unity are mingled with feelings of unease and nationalist paranoia, and threatened by the xenophobia of neo-fascists all over Europe. The questions of who and what is European have raised racist suspicions about difference. There is widespread anxiety because every attempt to determine what is European has to include a definition of what it is not. To the nationalist the removal of boundaries is a frightening, even painful, experience. Newness implies a loss of historical sovereignty and national identity. The general disquiet which opposes the ideal of a new Europe hinders an evaluation of Europe's past and future relationship to the 'other'.

Europeans are being asked to be specific about a definition which for centuries they have accepted in broad and general terms. The concept of Europeanness was unspecified before 1993; it required no qualification. Today that concept is much more tightly defined in political terms. Ultra-right nationalists want this tightness to resemble the skin of a sausage that protects its contents from contamination (the 'Kulturwurst' definition of culture). They want a fortress Europe, whose cultures are ethnically specific and whose visual arts are bound to particular classical traditions.

The leading arts institutions have neither the authority nor the wish to attempt such a rigid definition of the arts; nor are they yet prepared to redefine what is 'European' about them. There are official responses to the question of a European identity, but they appear inadequate when scrutinised in the context of European history, and when applied to the development of contemporary culture. The making of a nation's cultural history is always be a process of interweaving complex patterns of similarity and difference.[3] To contemplate identities on the premise of ethnic purity is factually inaccurate and distasteful in the context of European anti-semitism and the civil strife in regions such as the former Yugoslavia.

The notion that syncretism (the fusion of similarities) and hybridity (the creation of a third and novel possibility out of two disparate elements) are essential ingredients in the making of the modern nation state has become a distinguishing feature of much post-modernist thought. This suggests that cultural growth may be rhizomatic, like a ginger root with many points of origin, instead of being tap rooted, with a central and fixed growth system.[4]

One official response to the work of new European artists was the exhibition 'Das Andere Land' in West Berlin in 1986.[5] Dr Michael Haerdter, who helped to conceive the exhibition, wrote retrospectively of its failure to tackle the 'unresolved contradiction'[6] of trying to make the art and the artists a part of something that through circumstance they could not belong to. The 'something' he speaks of is evidently the national culture. The semantics of the title of this officially sponsored exhibition signalled that there were those who belonged to the nation (Das Land) and those who existed in another land (Das Andere Land), a conceptually different space, within the terrain of the West German Federal Republic.

Under German law, citizenship is a question of blood lineage and the passport one holds. An individual is either foreign or German; the constitution is clear about this, but not about how to define that individual's contribution to culture. Haerdter also points out that the difficulty of accepting the innovation and vitality of others, as building blocks in a nation's culture, is not novel to our time. Berlin accepted three hundred thousand Russian refugees between the years 1924 and 1928. There were six Russian banks, three daily newspapers and eighty-seven publishing concerns serving this vast community. Berlin's district of Charlottenburg was colloquially known as Charlottengrad. Some of Russia's greatest artists spent an important part of their lives there and enriched the cultural life of the city. Yet this has not really become a feature of the city's cultural history, nor of that of the nation. The reason it was difficult then, and remains so today, is the refusal by art historians and cultural critics to acknowledge the interdependence of cultural influences and to recognise the reciprocal element in all forms of cultural exchange.

It would be wrong to suggest that this myopia was an exclusively German problem, which it is not. This attitude exists in most of Europe's art institutions. In Britain in the Sixties, for example, it militated against a true understanding of the contribution made by many artists from the Commonwealth.[7] This changed in the Eighties, when the Arts Council sought the authentic dialogue which Paul Ricoeur claims to be essential as a means of dispelling our modernist scepticism. It replaced the notions of supremacy with partnership:

> When we discover that there are several cultures instead of just one and consequently at the time that we acknowledge the end of a sort of cultural monopoly, be it illusory or real, we are threatened with the destruction of our own discovery. Suddenly it becomes possible that there are just *others*, that we ourselves are an 'other' among others.[8]

It is important for us to make the step from domination to being 'just another other', if the 'new European' artist is to be included in mainstream developments. The French, for example, have traditionally shown a strong interest in the visual art of other peoples, from Wifredo Lam to the present. However, a debate about cultural difference with the dynamism to challenge the colonialist perception that views artists from the former colonies as displaced Frenchmen struggling to become integrated into the grand French tradition, has not emerged. Much that goes on in Paris tends to suggest that its cosmo-politanism has established itself in the national consciousness. Alas, the diversity which makes the capital such a wonderful place is largely absent from
its officially sponsored visual arts. The emphasis has been on integration into the national culture, and not on diversity within it. This policy asks all of the 'other' and very little of the French. Their engagement with diversity and difference is marked by tolerance and absorption. This has made many artists apprehensive that cultural difference has merely become fashionable because of the profile given it in a reluctant art world by the current, visionary Minister of Culture and Education.

The leading state museums and galleries, in France and elsewhere, should be eager to take a lead on the question of a new European cultural identity, but they are not. Their indifference to questions of diversity and reciprocity in the arts is echoed by the commercial galleries and the art academies. 'New European' artists seldom find employment as teachers or have their work shown and collected. It is not surprising that there is a pervasive belief that artists such as those included in this exhibition either do not exist or are not representative of the cultures in which they currently live.

Recent exhibitions in The Netherlands[9] have begun to challenge this view and to steer the debate about the national culture in the direction of diversity, syncretism and the individual identity of the artists who contribute to it. One hopes that this will continue not only in Holland but all over Europe, and that better exhibition strategies and innovative curatorship will make these issues seem more meaningful to the lives of ordinary people. We have to desist from marginalising 'otherness' by defining it as foreign, exotic, magical and extraordinary. As Guy Brett has commented,[10] European artists are never called upon to prove their Europeanness or to demonstrate their closeness to their cultural roots. Exhibitions should recognise difference where it exists and use it to broaden our understanding of art as it is practised today. Curators have the power to challenge predominant beliefs and explore alternative discourses, strategies and practices which might disclose the mainstream's open-mindedness (or lack of it).

Our desire to affirm the future identity of Europe should be accompanied by a willingness to investigate these complex matters of diversity and difference. We should free ourselves of outmoded, paternalistic attitudes and traditional concerns with racial lineage, permits and passports. Our focus in the search for newness should be on reciprocity and innovation. The experience of looking at any work of art can be described as a set of visual, mental and emotional manoeuvres which allow the viewer to establish a relationship to the work and the artist. Looking becomes a sensory exploration of a piece of unfamiliar territory; the visual experience as a reconnaissance – the work of art serving as a map and model for the mind, inviting inspection, recollection and discovery.

For artists, the creation of a work of art involves a similar set of manoeuvres. Constant discovery, recollection and inspection locate the position from which they launch their imagination into the real world. Possessed with the lonely courage to explore uncharted experience, they learn to negotiate their position within a culture. Their creative actions are imbued with a spirit of enterprise and open-mindedness which enables both the transgression of the old and the making of new frontiers. Like Columbus they have explored the edges of the known world, and it is their discoveries we seek to place before an open-minded audience. In this way we would hope to contribute towards transforming the imagined post-modern space into a tangible experience.

FOOTNOTES

1) Paul Ricoeur 'Universal Civilisation and National Cultures' , *History and Truth*, trans. Charles A. Kelbley, Evanston, North Western University Press, 1965, p.283.

2) From the 100 artist investigated and 35 studio visits made by Roger Malbert, Elizabeth Macgregor and myself, came the 11 in this exhibition.

3) Stuart Hall 'Our Mongrel Selves', New Statesman, September 1992

4) 'Rhizome – fragments' by Gilles Deleuze and Félix Guttari *Rhizome* cat. 1991. The authors have taken the principles of biological (plant) growth and applied it to philosophy. (A rhizome is a rootstock, like a ginger root that grows in a multiple growth system.) They set out six principles which outline the characteristics of a rhizome. The key difference between the centred, or tap root logic and rhizomatic logic is that the first is a trace of something that has fixed rules of growth, arising from a traditional core of knowledge, while the second is a form of map making, a process of creative and novel description of knowledge as it arises. Applying this to cultural development, there are tap rooted cultures and rhizomatic cultures. The first uses knowledge from a fixed or centred source, the second develops cultural knowledge through experimentation.

5) 'Das Andere Land' (Berlin, Edition Deplana, 1986)

6) Michael Haerdter 'Künstler in einem anderen Land' *Dokumentation 31 Loccumer Protokolle 03/87.*

7) See Rasheed Araeen's comments on this period of British art history in the chapter 'In the Citadel of Modernism' in the catalogue 'The Other Story'(London, Hayward Gallery, 1991).

8) Paul Ricoeur, op. cit., p.278.

9) 'Het Klimaat' a group of exhibitions organised by the Culturele Raad Zuid-Holland in 1991.
'Double Dutch' Stichting Kunst Mondial, Tilburg, Holland, 1991
'Rhizome' Haags Gemeentemuseum, Holland, 1991

10) Guy Brett 'Transcontinental' (London, Verso, Ikon Gallery and Cornerhouse. 1990).

MAHDJOUB BEN BELLA

Mahdjoub Ben Bella was born in Maghnia, Algeria. He lives and works in Tourcoing, France. He studied at the Ecole des Beaux-Arts in Oran, Algeria, and in Tourcoing and Paris. He participated in the activities – debates and exhibitions – of the Atelier de la Monnaie between 1969 and 1976. From 1978 to 1980 he taught at the Ecole des Beaux Arts, Cambrai. Recent projects include 'L'Envers du Nord', a road fresco on the Paris-Roubaix route (12 km), 1986, and murals painted for the ciné-théâtre d'Auchel (Pas-de-Calais) and at Riberac (Dordogne), 1987. Recent one-person exhibitions include 'La Souverainté des Signes', Centre Culturel Noroit, Arras, 1991.

List of works

Cageot peint 1 (Crate Paint 1)
Acrvlic on wood 64 x 54 cm

Cageot peint 2 (Crate Paint 2)
Acrvlic on wood 64 x 54 cm

Ecritures-peintes (Painted Writing)
Acrylic on canvas 115 x 89 cm,
115 x 89 cm, 130 x 97 cm,
130 x 97 cm

CARLOS CAPELAN

Carlos Capelán was born in Montevideo, Uruguay in 1948. He has lived in Lund, Sweden, since 1974. He studied at the Art School of Forum, Malmö, Sweden, 1978-81. Recent one-person exhibitions include Galerie El Patio, Bremen, 1987; Massachusetts School of Art, Boston, 1987 and 1988; L'Espace Latinoaméricaine, Paris 1988; Third Havana Biennal, Cuba, 1989 (Major award); One Twentyeight Gallery, New York, 1990; Galerie Basta, Hamburg, 1991; Galerie Hertz, Bremen, 1992; Subte Municipal, Montevideo, Uruguay, 1992; Lunds Konsthall, 1992. Performances include 'The Silent Word'; 'The Culture Night', Lund, 1987; Galerie El Patio, Bremen, 1989; Malmö Konsthall, 1992.

List of works

Installation 1993
Stones, books, earth, ink, bottles, burned books, lamps and other objects

BENNI EFRAT

Benni Efrat was born in Beirut in 1936. He lives and works in Antwerp. He has worked in a variety of media, including sculpture, performance, film and video. Recent one-person exhibitions include 'Heat Death, 2039' in Tel Hai, Israel, 1990; Elisabeth Franck Gallery, Knokke, 1991; Aleph Contemporary Arts, Almere-Nederland, 1991; Museum van Hedendaagse Kunst, Antwerp, 1991.

List of works

Ararat Express Oct. 2043 1986
Videotape

CHOHREH FEYZDJOU

Chohreh Feyzdjou was born in Teheran, Iran in 1955. She has lived and worked in Paris since 1975. She studied drawing and painting at the Beaux-Arts in Paris and aesthetics at the Sorbonne. One-person shows include 'New Experiences in America', Hourian Art Galleries, Oakland, California, 1987; 'Installation des objets sur planches', Ecole des Hautes Etudes en Sciences Sociales, Paris, 1988; 'Products of Chohreh Feyzdjou 1988-92', Galerie Patricia Dorfmnn, Paris 1992; 'Découvertes', 1993, Paris, Galerie Renate Schröder, Cologne, 1993. Her work was acquired by the Fonds National d'Art Contemporain (1990).

List of works

Products of Chohreh Feyzdjou 1988-1992
Mixed media installation
Wax, pigment, thread, steel wire, animal hide, plastic, cord, sugar, carbon, wool, cotton, feathers, fleece, wood, paper, glass jars, gouache, elastic bands, gum, nails, cardboard, canvas, videotape

CLAUDIO GOULART

Claudio Goulart was born in Porto Alegre, Brazil in 1954. He has lived in Amsterdam since 1976. He studied art and architecture and his work takes a variety of forms, including photography, performance, video, installation, set design and cable television. Recent exhibitions include Performance Festival, de Lantaren, Rotterdam, 1984; World Wide Video Festival, Kijkhuis, The Hague; Poetry International, De Doelen, Rotterdam, 1986; Stadsschouwburg, Amsterdam, 1987; De Watertoren, Vlissingen, 1991; De Oude Kerk, Amsterdam, 1992.

List of works

VALE QUANTO PESA
IT'S WORTH ITS WEIGHT 1993
Mixed media installation

YING LIANG

Ying Liang was born in 1961 in Peking. She studied at Guang Zhou Art School in China and then at the Fine Art School in Hamburg, Germany. She now lives and works in Hamburg. She has exhibited in Germany and elsewhere since 1985. Her most recent exhibitions were at Galerie Basta, Hamburg, and Hong Kong Art Centre, Hong Kong. She has drawings in the collection of Carl and Carin Vogel, Hamburg.

List of works

Don't be too glad, beware, tomorrow you may have green shit. . . 1989
Ink on paper 45 x 50 cm

I should really write to you 1989
Ink on paper 44 x 48 cm

Revolution is no invitation to dinner 1989
Ink on paper 44 x 48 cm

Family tree 1990
Ink on paper 43 x 48 cm

Flowered pants for Mrs Liu 1990
Ink on paper 48 x 44 cm

If the broom doesn't sweep away the dust... 1990
Ink on paper 44 x 48 cm

Pencil-wife 1990
Ink on paper 44 x 49 cm

Self 1990
Ink on paper 43 x 43 cm

Water buffalo 1991
Ink on paper 43 x 48 cm
Hans Hillgruber, Hamburg

Untitled 1990
Ink on paper 44 x 48 cm
Galerie Basta, Hamburg

Untitled 1990
Ink on paper 44 x 48 cm

Untitled 1990
Ink on paper 44 x 48 cm

Untitled 1990
Ink on paper 44 x 48 cm

Little car, beep, beep, beep, in it sits big Mao... 1991
Ink on paper 43 x 49 cm

My son will be a genius 1991
Ink on paper 45 x 50 cm

Untitled 1991
Ink on paper 44 x 48 cm
Hans Hillgruber, Hamburg

Untitled 1991
Ink on paper 44 x 48 cm

Untitled 1991
Ink on paper 20 x 20 cm

Mosquitos in Hang-Zhou 1991
Ink on paper 20 x 20 cm

Untitled 1991
Ink on paper 20 x 20 cm

Man cooking 1991
Ink on paper 20 x 20 cm

LEA LUBLIN

Lea Lublin was born in Argentina. She is a naturalised French subject and lives and works in Paris. Since 1977 she has taught at the Sorbonne. She received a research scholarship from the John Simon Guggenheim Foundation, New York, 1984-5, and a commission from the Centre National des Arts Plastiques, 1985. Recent one-person exhibitions include 'Le dessin du désir', Galerie del Retiro, Buenos Aires, 1980; 'Le Strip-tease de l'enfant-dieu', Galerie Yvon Lambert, Paris; 'Le porte-cierges trouvé objet perdu de Marcel Duchamp', Abbaye de Graville, Le Havre, 1989; 'Lea et les signes', Galerie Pierre Bernard, Nice, 1990; 'Présent suspendu – Marcel Duchamp 1919-1991 – objets perdus/objets trouvés', Centre Regional d'Art Contemporain Midi-Pyrénés, Labège-Innpole. Hôtel des Arts, Fondation Nationale des Arts, Paris, 1991.

List of works

La Bouteille perdue de Marcel Duchamp, l'affichette, l'étiquette (The Lost Bottle of Marcel Duchamp, the Poster, the Label) 1991
Nine boxed back-lit transparencies from a series of fifteen

AS M'BENGUE

Ibrahima M'Bengue, aka As, was born in Dakar, Senegal in 1959. He has lived in Paris since 1982. He studied at the Ecole des Beaux-Arts in Dakar and then at the Beaux-Arts in Paris. Since 1990 he has worked in a studio at the Hôpital Ephémère, Paris, where he had his first solo exhibition in 1991. He has since had one-person shows at the Grand Palais and Albert Benamou Galleries in Paris, Barbara Pensoy and Michael Lang in New York, and Dany Keller Galerie in Munich.

List of works

Une semaine de bonté, ou les trois éléments capitaux Max E (A Week of Kindness, or the Three Essential Elements of Max E)
1992
Oil on canvas 100 x 130 cm

La femme. 100 têtes (The Woman. 100 Heads) 1992
Oil on canvas 100 x 130 cm

Le musée visite de l'homme... Notre Dame de Paris (The Man's Museum Visit...)
1992
Oil on canvas 190 x 200 cm

Les malheurs des immortels. 3 hommes libres (The Misfortunes of the Immortals. 3 Free Men) 1992
Oil on canvas 100 x 130 cm

Bibliothéque litteraire
(Literary Library) 1992
Oil on canvas 100 x 130 cm

Une balance dans l'histoire naturelle (A Balance in Natural History) 1992
Oil on canvas 100 x 130 cm

FLAVIO PONS

Flavio Pons was born in Dom Pedrito, Brazil in 1947. He has lived in Amsterdam since 1975. He studied architecture from 1968 to 1971, after which he worked as an environmental artist in Rio de Janeiro. He has used various techniques and media during his career, including woodcuts, environments, collages, assemblages, performance, installation, photography and video. Recently he has shown mainly video, installations and sculpture. Recent exhibitions include Performance Festivals in Bracknell and de Lantaran, Rotterdam in 1985; Time-Based Arts, Amsterdam, 1986; Het Prinsenhof, Delft, 1988; Suzanne Biederberg Gallery, Amsterdam, 1991; Theatre an de Werf, Utrecht, 1992.

List of works

Solids 1993
Mixed media installation

FELIX DE ROOY

Felix de Rooy was born in Curaçao, the Dutch Antilles. He lives in Amsterdam. A painter, theatre and film director, he received his fine arts training at the Psychopolis Academy of the Plastic Arts in The Hague. He worked as an art teacher and cultural civil servant in Curaçao, where he won the Cola Debrot prize. He has exhibited his art in Santo Domingo, Mexico, Surinam, the Dutch Antilles and the Netherlands. In 1976 he founded the theatre company 'Cosmic Illusion Productions' with Norman de Palm. In 1982 he received his Master's Degree in Film and Television Directing from the University of New York. His major feature films are Desirée (1984), Almcita Soul of Desolato (1986), and Ava & Gabriel (1990).

List of works

Death becomes him 1992
Mixed media collage 90 x 112 cm

Noche buena, mala noche/Battle of the Sexes 1991
Mixed media collage 55 x 150 cm

Resurrection 1990
Mixed media collage 127 x 127 cm

Caribbean Nostalgia 1988
Mixed media collage 68 x 110 cm

Cry Surinam 1992
Mixed media assemblage
110 x 68 x 68 cm

Ave Europa Regina/White on Black 1991
Mixed media assemblage
43 x 69 x 21 cm

Primal Mother 1993
Mixed media assemblage

OHANNES TAPYULI

Ohannes Tapyuli is Armenian, born in Kangal, Turkey in 1944, and now lives in Braunschweig, Germany. He studied at the Kunstakademie, Stuttgart, 1966-71, and taught at the Hochschule für Bildende Künste, Braunschweig, 1971-9. He has been awarded prizes for art from the cities of Braunschweig and Nordhorn (1979), from the Sprengel Stiftung (1981) and Villa-Massimo (1981). He lived in Malaga, Spain, 1980-4, and Rome, 1984-5.

List of works

We Are Rich 1992
6 of 12 frames
Paper collage on board
192 x 136 cm each